The Insane Poets

DAVID ROLLINS

JULIE STACEY

DAVID PARKIN

GREEN CAT BOOKS

Published in 2020 by
GREEN CAT BOOKS
19 St Christopher's Way
Pride Park
Derby
DE24 8JY
www.green-cat.co

DEDICATION

To Mum. I miss you.

Julie Stacey

For my parents' love, understanding and stamina.

David Parkin

Rachael Lawrence, my soulmate.

David Rollins

CONTENTS

CONTENTS

CONTENTS

CONTENTS

The Most Delicious Topping

What a relief!
Depression has fallen away.
Along with all the grief.
Replaced with life's beauty and
metaphorical wings,
and the most delicious topping of self-
belief.
There is the sweetest of sounds that my
soul sings.
I have incredible confidence.
I will live my life in beauty with opulence.

My high this time is here to stay!
Incredible skills,
Strengths,
Intelligence
will no longer fade away.
I can almost read minds too,
communicate with those long gone
through the journey of death,
As one day

all of mankind will be able to do.

I stride around in my golden gown.
Upon my head I wear my jewelled crown.
No longer stumbling about,
looking like a fucked-up clown.
I know my dreams will come true.
So confident am I.
All I need to do is push forward.
No procrastination.
Give life a try.

Julie Stacey

Chaos

The universal noise
Typified by the
Big bang origin
And its chaotic
Pattern of expanding
Suns and planets
All dust and ice
Gas swirling
Moving away
From the chaotic
planet housing
bacteria and traffic
phones and weeds
foaming sea
haphazard bits
of land shapes
covered in odd
viral organisms
all arms and legs
noisy movement
spreading, growing

destroying

creating

its own big bang

its discovery of

destructive atom

and mushroom explosion

unsatisfying

in its madness

choosing not expansion

instead implosion

of would-be gods

manufactured

viral chaos.

David Rollins

Forest of Mystery

Deep within the forest of mystery
a face appeared,
from behind the ancient tree.
It was Lady Jane Grey,
spilling golden light tears.
as she said to me,
"I'm not really dead,
although I lost my head.
I was only a kid,
when made ruler of this
land.
Nine days it was,
until their command,
to throw me to
the guillotine's deadly hand.
Yet consider this,
I was then set free
from a musky, dark tower,
as you can be,
when you claim your power.

A life then lived
full of positivity.
No wasting away
with rotten anxiety."
Her face then
disappeared, behind that
ancient tree and I walked
away, feeling pleasantly
weird.

Julie Stacey
Pic by Julie Stacey

Library Assistant

Sunshine filters through the space
Between the window and me.
The fan's switched on
And my glass empty.

I sit typing tickets.
Is this all there is?
Is there nothing more
than sitting at a desk all day
asking impossible questions
Of my typewriter?

David Rollins

A Familiar Story

I am glad the pain has eased.

When from my bipolar,

you decided to be released.

Wrenching the key back from my heart.

The one you gave me in a time,

before you made a fresh start.

Leaving me with a familiar story.

Loneliness, with fleeting love and glory.

Julie Stacey

Running

In these troubled times,
more often than not
I find
that I am happiest whilst running.

And it makes me feel a little sad,
because it's a lonely thing to do.
But the grins at the dinner parties
and the mugs in the pubs
only make me nervous.
So I lace up my jogging shoes
and choose music on my faithful cheap,
knackered and battered MP3.
And at the moment it's the drinkers, the
sluggers, the fighters,
who are singing to me.
Old poets who have been there
and then come back.
I seem to need to know their stories.
And as I bounce beside the river,
it's like a score, a fantastic soundtrack,
as the music moves with my world.

A cracked voice falters,
Gently unfurls,
Sighs down the chords,
Two gulls dip to the water
Then soar,
Away, away and high.
And it's beautiful,
I wonder
did God have music in mind when he taught
them how to fly?

And other such thoughts as I pant heavily by
and stop and rewind
a verse that I love,
and listen again,
and watch the stillness of the heron,
the steel-backed black moorhen.

And I'm happy.

I need this journey,
Especially the halfway point,
where,

heart pounding,

I stop,

bend,

breath,

slowly turn upon my tracks,

and with legs aching, chest heaving,

I follow the flow of the river home,

and I know,

that I have been there,

and that I can make it back.

David Parkin

When Words Go Blind

When words go blind
I sit there
and in vain,
I try and read your mind,
whilst hating mine.
It never grasps the future,
only scraps with the past.
So what's the point in trying to understand
your secrets,
when I can't understand mine.
I only know
there's not much time
between you and I.
I just can't see it
when words go blind.

                                        Julie Stacey

The Rotting Corpse

The rotting corpse
Of my dreams
Carried from childhood
to its death, its slow, painful death
has at its very core
a knife in its back.

The rotting corpse
died eventually,
Snuffed out by vodka and Diazapam,
Destroyed by my ambition
hung by my lacking,
by my inability to see inside.

The rotting corpse
Failed to survive
Even when I did, resuscitated unwillingly.
I had a dream, an altruism,
Forgetting my daily mantra
'Never forget that people are twats'
I hoped, and in my hope I forgot.

The rotting corpse
Has been fed on over time
By me, unable to see clearly,
By you, your selfish desires and actions
Quite rightly unable to see mine,
By the powers on Earth,
Corrupt, self-serving powers,
Democracy turned to fascism,
Quite wrongly unwilling to see mine.
And let down, stabbed and then eaten up
The rotting corpse dies,
Leaving only anger, and self-righteous rage.
The rotting corpse of my dreams
Awaits me, draws me and blinds me,
I come, my dreams, I come.

David Rollins

Mr Mania

Mr Mania is like a bad lover
who treats me like a queen
and tells me
for my lows and anxiety,
he holds the vaccine.

I just can't sleep,
as he holds me so tight.
So we dance and sway,
the night away
and he tells me this time,
he is here to stay.

With kisses so dangerous
I take leave of my senses
"Don't worry,"
he whispers,
"I will take care of all your expenses."

He takes me to breakneck heights,
showing me so many unbelievable sights.

Giving me liberty in his rocket,
as he slips a golden star in my pocket,
and tenderly kisses my bipolar locket.

My ecstasy entwines with his,
so intense,
that it separates me from my
common sense.
But he shrugs and insists
I possess sixth sense.

I am so excited,
I talk and talk,
friends turn
away from me
and away they walk.
They don't care
for this love affair.
But they are not here,
they are over there.
Another reality,
so magic
they are unaware.

But the time soon comes,
and I have been dropped,
I can barely life my bruised head from the
stone-cold floor.
How quick Mr Mania
does turn very cruel.
With him he takes my spiritual sight, skills
wit, confidence and the talents I thought
I had.
With my head in my hands,
I just sit and sit.
Overwhelmed by dread.
Thoughts tormenting my head.
Family, friends and strangers.
To them,
the abusive and strange things
I have said.

All I want to do now is hide in my bed,
allowing apathy to rule.
Because I am the galactic fool.

My belief was so strong,
that with him a spiritual
awaking.
Now everything has gone
wrong,
now he has gone,
leaving his last gift,
of mental agony.
All I can see,
creeping forward,
is the terror of anxiety.
And feeling so damned low!
Yet despite my family's hate,
I want to see him again.
It's just a matter of when.
So for his visits,
I still wait.

Julie Stacey
Pic by Jessica Stacey

Profundity

Whenever I have a breakdown,
I turn it into art,
A bit like that boy at school,
Who was so very proud of his farts.

David Parkin

Eggs-ercise

It has no arms, it has no legs.
It's not quite round or oval,
and if you push it down a hill
eggs-ercise will makes it scowl.

Its whites indeed are full of fat,
and yet it has no belly.
If you suggest it eggs-ercise,
it'll think you are quite funny.

The only thing that it can do,
(its yellow liquid)... running,
so if you were to call it fat,
it'd think that you were punning.

David Rollins

The Worst Lie

At your funeral, Mum,
I found it hard to cry.
So numb was I.
Mania had been cruel, you
see.
Telling me the worst lie.
You were special like me
and despite cancer,
they would heal you.
You would live not die.
Did I deserve disappointment so
intense, pulling my heart out with its
savage wrench?
Its intent,
a bitter coldness
to resent your departure
and you.
For taking
your unconditional love away from me.

Within my grief,
I was angry, you see.
How selfish of me.

Julie Stacey
Pic by Julie Stacey

I Don't Remember the Fall

Did I step gently?
Or was it all scramble
To catch up to the racing brain?
My slippered feet, neat, forever on the
edge.

Did I look to the sea and smile?
Or perhaps it was black with rain,
Did I look to the sea and did I cry?
The punctured clouds wracked with pain.

But it is no use,
I cannot see it,
I don't remember the fall.
It is blocked,
Lost in the infinity of my mind.

On my ribs, on my throat, on my heart,
I have scars where the bones shattered,
But still,
I don't remember the fall.   David Parkin

Peace

The space between
That solid stuff
The dark matter peace
Of nothingness between.
The focussed gaze
Of open eyes,
Barely blinking
Gazing from behind
Translucent glass,
At the roads and fields
The no noise birds
The no noise traffic
The stillness
Of face and body
Not daring to move
In the sudden second long
Peace of the universe.
Mirroring its slow, quiet nature.
The universe inside the still gazing eyes
Distant and daring unable to look away

David Rollins

Ghost Town Head

People don't want to come near
and looking back at my madness
I can understand why they steer clear.
Humiliation holding my hand,
with the most agonising fear.
Chattering away.
"You can't escape your thoughts,"
I hear it say.
The only sound
in my ghost town head.

The torment
It's more intense,
as it's back to work today.
Three months of being away.
Thoughts of facing people,
second guessing
of what their thoughts of me say.
So I take Diazepam,
wrap myself in a quilt
to sleep on the sofa instead.

My second bed.
But that's all part of living
with a ghost town head.

Julie Stacey

Outside

I see myself
Inside my mind
Outside, outsider
Silhouette
Against the dark night
The tall buildings
And me
Standing small
Alone even here.
Within the image
I see

David Rollins

Dreams

Dreams.
They take us anywhere
within the existence of timeless.
So let's dream together
in eternal bliss,
for inner peace,
is all that I wish.

Julie Stacey

When I Was Gentle, When I Was Kind

Long ago there was a time
When I was gentle,
When I was kind,
Then one day I lost my mind,
And have forever since been running blind,
So that now with open eyes I find,
I cannot see,
Hear,
Touch,
Or even taste the time,
When I was gentle,
When I was kind.

David Parkin

Eastern Moon

Let's fly to the moon my dear friend,
and see the earth spin
whilst sitting with spirit.
Just watching.
We will see Eastern Park
and give thanks,
that living is breathing
and so much more.

Julie Stacey

The Question of Faith

Wearing just a bed sheet,
Eyes large and blank,
Plague thin,
He held out his hand,
Like some Ethiopian saint,
Hoping to bless us,
The NHS bouncers,
Soon took him away,
To a madder ward.

Another boy,
Who was deaf and spoke in tongues,
Held my hands,
And recited a poem.
The fish in the sea,
the birds in the sky.
It was simple,
But I felt a rush up my arms,
Filling the head,
And I felt like I was blessed.
And some mornings,

While I fed the wagtails bread,
I felt like I could see,
The birds
The sky,
The sea,
Something other,
Passing through me.

Then the day began at nine,
Form an orderly line,
Peppered with saints and prophets,
To collect their morning medication.

David Parkin

Kitty Kitty (True Story)

"Here, kitty kitty,"
the voice called from the hall
Such an evil laugh,
as my cat sat staring at the wall.
My body went cold.
With each tick of the clock,
I turned to stone.
I could not move,
as my cig burnt down,
My mind dripped ice-cold water
down my spine.
That night
I sat there all alone,
in my silent home.

Half an hour had passed
when I crept across
the carpeted floor,
as I anxiously planned,
a run for the front door.
Then something sparked in my head.

Anger took over instead.
This is my territory!
I'm not letting evil get to me.
And my cat still sat there
staring at that wall.

Then I remembered the protective power
It's in us all
It stilled my mind
while telling me,
I'm still alone here tonight.
My sixth sense was right
as I checked each room,
with a heightened sight.
There was no one.
No one at all!
I swear that night
I heard the devil call.

Julie Stacey

White Coffin

The sorrow of the chalk white coffin
I stare out of the dark window
Seeing the rain bouncing off the road
Wondering if a different book had been
written
If that ticking clock stopped
If the dark rain ceased
If sorrow itself would die
Would you be safe?
If sorrow itself would die
If the dark rain ceased
If that ticking clock stopped
Wondering if a different book had been
written
Seeing the rain bouncing off the road
I stare out of the dark window
The sorrow of the chalk white coffin

David Rollins

Landing on Your Head

When I came round I was giggling,
After jumping off a roof.
Broken boned and dribbling,
I was living proof,
That the injured brain can "suffer" from
euphoria,
Which brightens your hospital bed.
So be aware that if you want to jump to
your death,
You might feel differently if you land on
your head.

David Parkin

Ocean of Misery

I am so desperate!
But they don't understand.
I am lost in a polluted sea.
It's called the Ocean of Misery.
Most days I feel like I am drowning,
It's hard to breath,
so I tend to sleep
my only relief.

I am scared to go out!
Afraid of this constant shout,
going on in my head.
My anxious thoughts voicing

opinions.

People will look at me,
disgusted in what they see.
Is my sentence for life?
I struggle,
hopelessly.
Gasping for breath.
It's terrifying, living in my head.

That tells me,

over and over,

my mind they will always hold.

So I lay there,

longing to be old.

Yet I want friends,

a partner,

confidence

and a job too!

Not this feeling of incompetence!

"Please someone",

I inwardly beg,

"tell me what to do"

But nobody can hear my thoughts,

that demand to them I be true.

They grip my back,

I struggle to swim.

Will I ever win

This anchor of fear.

Keeping me here.

Lost, so dreadful and cold.

In the Ocean of Misery.

Julie Stacey
Pic by Julie Stacey

Twins

I envied his calm
and he envied my chaos
If only we'd talked.

He got a new job
His life always going well
Not the crazy twin

Sat drinking coffee
We laugh over something daft
Random twin humour

My first suicide
A large bottle of vodka
My twin saving me

My twin visits me.
The confused mental health nurse
Mistakes him for me.

He's a therapist.

I write poetry and stuff.

That's how we both deal.

David Rollins

Mania's Clarity

Nobody believes,
that I can see the spirits
connected to our souls.
So I keep quiet most of the time,
hoping machine guns wont chime
and death tolls add up, deep into the mine.
Coal long gone.
Yet the ancient crystals sparkle their love
with sharp edges dripping our blood.

The ignorant ignore what the enlightened
say.
We can all own an ecstasy of peace.
Once known,
even if it comes and goes,
within the darkness,
hope always glows.

I search for this oasis
where a mysterious force,
welcomes humanity to a beautiful light.

I wish they could awaken
and own their sight.

Julie Stacey

Photo Call

That boy standing still
In the 'far too big' garden
Dwarfed by bigger aunts
Demanding a pose
And ignoring the big fear
Of the too small child

David Rollins

Only Two Days

It had only been two days that my
depression had lifted
when I realised that unknown to most,
mankind is beautifully gifted.
My body is perfectly aligned.
Connecting me to a higher flow of mind.
But a window is left open,
unprotected,
psychosis silently woken.
Tapping my shoulder,
I am secretly selected,
To be taken on an exhilarating lift,
A reality,
craftily making me feel oh so rich.
Mania is the strangest night shift.

Julie Stacey

Split

A dead man follows me.
He had the strength to hold that first
heartbreak,
He did not drown it with drink,
He did not forget it with pills,
And while there may have been tears,
It did not crack him open,
Exposed and tender,
To the coming years.

He does not fear love.

Not every day but most,
In the setting sun the dead man grows,
And in the oncoming dusk,
He casts me like a shadow.

David Parkin

Depression

Dead senses stifle my
Eyes, so I gaze lazily upon
People. I mark but don't mark their
Reactions. Their very lives
Escape from my memory, not even
Scarred across its reality soft
Surface. It feels as though nothing matters
In this sublime, decayed world. No
Observation has any meaning, but
Nihilism.

David Rollins

I'm awake

I can't sleep.
Maybe now I can
as I wait for the sun to
rise.
Is it okay to sleep
outdoors?
Neighbours to hear my
snores.
I think it is
as they're asleep and I'm
awake
I have little shoulders and
hands and they may worry that
I'm mad!
Yet at this time I am not sad,
as they snore in their own snot,
whilst dreaming in a murky lake.
I just long for sleep,
but not like them,
As they're asleep and I'm awake.

Julie Stacey

Pic by Jessica Stacey

A Few Haiku

I find politics
and most mental health issues
meet in the middle

————————————————————

I can feel anger bubbling,
Moving up onto my face,
Scowling tension.

————————————————————

So many people,
their noisy lives crossing mine,
leaving, then replaced.

David Rollins

Spread Those Wings

I forget myself and who I am.
but I try my best
to hate less.
It's not good to be angry,
nor bitter
and all those things.
We are all guilty of committing
stupidity's sins.

so I try to be good to others
and spread my dust-filled wings.
Surviving
Fighting
and striving to uncover a mystifying light
with beauty that holds clear insight.

Julie Stacey

I Know This

When I found him in the trees,
He looked at peace.
Eyes closed,
Seated,
Head gently resting forward.

Then a lurch,
A challenge to the eye,
He was not sitting,
His legs flat behind,
At a severe, obscene right angle.

Then I saw the cable,
Drawn tight behind his back,
Painting his face pale,
Pulling his chin to his chest.
Looking at him hurt my eyes,
He must have jumped to break the neck,
He was taller than the height that hung him.

There was no noose to loosen,

Just a tight ball of savage knots,
So the nurse on the phone told me,
That I'd have to cut him down.
She said that sentence so gently,
Then the snap and the thud as he hit the
ground,
With no trace of life left.
The gathered onlookers gasped as one,
At the ugly weight of death.

Afterwards in the pub,
My friends bought me drinks,
And commended me for so being brave.
Of all the people to find him hanging,
Not lovely troubled nutter Dave.

But as the weeks passed,
In a slowly clearing Zopiclone haze,
I was stunned to find that it had not broken
me,
I think because I understood,
Those thoughts, that feeling, those last
breaths,

When the mind demands nothing but
death.

I understood
Those thoughts,
So without hope,
So black,
In the moment are they the only thing to
answer to
I know this because I can look back,
I know this because those thoughts do, in
the end, pass.

The tragedy wasn't that he tried,
The tragedy was that he got it right.
I know this because every single day,
I close my eyes and give thanks,
Because when I tried,
I failed.

David Parkin

Don't Go into the Woods Today

Don't go into the woods today.
There are fiends there, not friends,
hiding.
They desire to kill you.
Too far gone
on evil's side.
Soon it will all begin
and at last you will say,
"oh my god no,
there must be another way."

They will rip you with their swords,
as they act like lords.
Or maybe an axe through your head,
as this is the way they were led.
They will sell some as slaves,
Dark souls they follow the Devil's way.
They don't care for people's lives
as they lick the blood dripping down
from their knives.
As evil rode down a path,

through thousands of years in
time. But you don't believe in this,
only the media you mime.

Julie Stacey

Spellcecker

A spllcecker's a wonerfull thing
I really wish I had ono
The joys that it coukd bring If
a spellchecker was the think
That I neaded
But I don't

David Rollins

In The Flow

When I am in the flow,
I just know,
I am the creator of my life.
I create my own strife,
I own my own power.
I no longer hide from life and cower.
A place where life exists.
Inner peace I no longer resist.
I no longer own a frown
on my deeply lined brow.
When I am in the flow,
The secrets of life,
do I know.

Julie Stacey

Wanking Under Section

Wanking under section,
Is a tricky thing to do.
You either do it in the showers,
Or sometimes on the loo.

Wanking in your room is risky,
Because regular nurse visits are standard,
You've got to bash the bishop quickly,
So you're not caught creamy-handed.

And there's no visual stimulation,
For patients wanting to cum,
The best thing you can hope for,
Is page three of The Sun.

So you fantasize about that pretty nurse,
Maybe in some kinky leather.
Or what about that junior doctor,
Or both of them together?

So it's very degrading for all involved,
From the nurses just doing their jobs,
To the poor porn-deprived mad men,
Just trying to knock one off.

So many freedoms are taken away,
When you are placed under section,
No privacy, no laptops and no filthy mags,
If they could they'd ban all erections.

So let the broken men buy their porn,
And allow them some privacy with their
cock,
Because wanking is a human right,
And just make sure the nurses knock.

David Parkin

Mind to Mind (True Story)

Betty Shine wrote Mind to Mind
She proved this by
Shaking my hand.
Breaking through my thoughts
with a clear voice she said,
"Hello to you, I am one too."
Yet at this time
I didn't know she was dead.
So the very next day
I googled her name.
And to be honest with you
She really came through
at a time
I was not insane.
Yesterday through my mind,
her soul she aligned.
Betty Shine
Wrote Mind to Mind.

Julie Stacey

Confusion

My brain now stretched out
A confusion of wire threads
Of thoughts tangled up

If I could just see
My multi-coloured thought strands
Could I sort them out?

Or are they best left
A mess of mixed sanity
And insanity?

A red, pink and white
Genius of creation
Floating in my head

David Rollins

Another World to be Found

Swimming in the orange sea
as deep as one could ever be.
There is another other world,
forever here to be found.
That's sure to astound.
With magnificent sights and sounds.
No blood bombs and war,
This really should be the way,
with another other world to be found.

Yet the world is crazy!
People are so very lazy,
to face the screams of truth.
Like it's okay to be aloof.
Tightening the noose of slavery
from the bringers of misery.
Control, power and greed,
These psychopaths holding on tight
to their soldiers with guns.
Who they order,
the killing of mother's sons.

Not caring of other's grief
Let's hope a time comes.
That here on Earth,
Mankind will eventually come together.
And realise
that separation is a cloak of illusion.
I think the reason we are here,
is spiritual evolution.

Julie Stacey

Attic Space

These are my rooms and yours.
Boxes with high walls.
Inside our individual heads.
Places where we keep and find thoughts

Work, friends, not friends,
places, likes, not likes,
Memories, good, not good,
Events, past, passed by
My thoughts, your thoughts

My rooms have arches of stone
Instead of wooden doors
That close and exclude
Everyone... except you
Because we are not different at all.

David Rollins

Things Have Changed

Ten years have passed since 2010,
My rules have changed a lot since then,
a time where I thought my life had come to
a head,
The ruler of my life was crisis and
depression.
So numb, only allowing fear
Now a rainbow shines with truths so clear
and I spend time with those so dear.
But many years I have lost
In cloud and dust.
Allowing my soul to dampen and rust.
A time of life with no hope, no drive.
However, lessons learned and move
forward I must.
Because happiness for myself I no longer
deprive.

Julie Stacey

A Maybe

When you live with suicide,
Not always,
But as a maybe,
It limits the risks you are willing to take
With other people's lives.

I don't want to leave a woman in black,
Or become a sad story when she's drunk,
With each telling,
I become more distant.
And perhaps the pain more precise.

I have forgotten the fiction of a child,
With the first two sleepless years,
Maybe I would have been a good father,
Yet I dread becoming someone's lost, dead
dad.
And so I turn my back on the heart of life.
On our meaning.

And so, I hope to outlive my parents.

I don't want to leave them with a hurt,

So raw,

So urgent,

So always sudden.

But I know when I fall they are at the centre
of my mind,

And it still is not enough to stop me.

When you live with suicide,

Not always,

But as a maybe.

David Parkin

<u>Within a Flow of Synchronicity</u>

What is it I can see,

within this flow of synchronicity?

It's so clear man could live in ecstasy.

As beauty resides within the psyche.

A hidden depth so loving and kind.

In the stillness of your mind,

turn the key and set your spirit free.

Then you will see what I can see

Julie Stacey

Never Put Your Finger in a Cat

Never put your finger in a cat,

Be it slim,

Siamese,

Or black and fat,

The type of feline is quite beside the fact.

Never put your finger in a cat.

David Parkin

Men in White Coats

Why do they use the term men in white
coats?
It's just women and men,
writing notes.
Same old questions,
of mood description.
It only helps them,
to choose a prescription.
Some not really caring
as in their eyes you see,
a flatness.
Their souls'
so bored.
So wearying,
with years
of mental illness stories.

And nurses!
They can be cold too.
Showing their contempt towards you.
We only want a cup of tea,

when we knock on the office door.
But most,
glance,
then turn their backs on us.
So my hospital friend trudges back to her
bed,
I go outside,
hide
and have a cigarette instead.
Breaking cruel rules.
No nicotine comfort,
dictatorship said.
For those locked up,
with a painful head.
so "jobsworths" watch patients
who go outside,
following those who head towards the
door.
Poor sods,
whose eyes only watch the floor.
downtrodden by life.
Their only bit of relief is to have a smoke.
I am telling you

taking that away from them,
their choices.
It's a fucking Joke.

Julie Stacey

When I Think of What We Did Last Night

When I think of what we did last night,
I can't help but sigh,
Then slowly puff my cheeks out,
And look toward the sky.

Then glancing down with a secret grin,
I slowly shake my head,
My heart throbs against its ribcage,
My cock against my leg.

David Parkin

Forced to Kneel

It's all distorted!
All we think is real.
As we are forced to kneel
and shuffle through life.
Fresh air we should breathe,
Instead of this leash.
Which makes our minds sink,
to sever the link,
to an awesome power and
beauty so fine.

The horrors we see
on the TV.
Normality.
The war's burning on,
while we chat on the net.
But it may not be long
before our way of life is long
gone.

Dictatorship we now see
and of course we agree
There's a killer disease
but was it made in their lab?
or is nature about to release, our
species,
so it can live in peace?

Julie Stacey

<u>Stranger</u>

I saw a girl outside the park
Carrying two carrier bags,
and wearing a bright red beret.
I said to myself
Is it . . .
No it can't be . . .
It looks like . . .
No, surely not . . .
Yes . . .
I'll go and intro . . .
She got on a bus.

David Rollins

Bipolar

Bipolar.
They think it's an illness
but it's a condition instead.
It holds universal power,
but it gets too much.
when you go too high
losing control,
madness then forms a destructive role.
When that journey begins
believe me, I can see the secrets of
creativity
and the way the world can be.
Then I fall down,
no connection,
no trust.
So like a wild horse
control it I must.

Julie Stacey

It's Not True

When the worst has, of course, happened
again,
And it feels like the only reality you ever
knew,
When all you can see is the blinkered pain,
I'm writing to tell you,
It's not true.

When every minute lasts an hour,
And the hurt in every second is so new,
When the blackened buds of depression
flower,
I'm writing to tell you,
It's not true.

When you're absolutely sure it's your time
to die,
And all hope has blankly disappeared from
view,
When the world breathes like a rotting sigh,
I'm writing to tell you,

It's not true.

I am writing from the future and the past,
I know you don't believe it but I am you,
So in this time of darkness please take
heart,
Because,
It's not true,
It's not true,
It's not true.

David Parkin

A Full Ashtray

Smoking,
Just looking around the room.
Same old books
and a full ashtray,
giving me dirty looks.
I wish that life could be different
and I could control my mind.
But mine just shakes and hides,
In the comfort of its den.
Dissociating,
whilst wanting to live.
Wanting to give.
But there's a horizontal mountain.
No door.
No garden gate.
Nor a fence to climb.
The only strength I have
is to make coffee,
that I sip,
as I constantly glance at the time.
with a head full of notes.

Maybe tomorrow I will eventually paint the
hall,
or follow my soul
on its daily call.

Julie Stacey

Terminal

This city is ill
Diseased by its populous
Smog lungs overwhelmed

The autumn weather
Gives my city the sniffles
Making its eyes weep

City heat follows
Then downpour like diarrhoea
Clears the putrid air

Till its sewers full
My city drowns in its mess
Spewing people waste

Its arteries clogged
By plastics, condoms, tampons.
Slowing down… stopping.

Its long death rattle

Strangling those inhabitants.
Murder, Suicide.

David Rollins

All These Things

If I could kiss away your sadness,
With all my heart,
With my soul
And with a grinding of hips,
I would snog a big smile across your lips.
If I could catch your tears,
I would collect them in cups,
With a Blue Peter bonanza
Of cotton wool and eggs,
I would water and dote
On a thousand cress heads.
With concentration,
A million felt tips,
With creased brow
And a childish tongue sticking out through
my lips,
I would create a green-haired army
Stretching a mile.
If it would make your day,
If it would make you smile.
If I could take my hope,

I would build him wings,
Made from tea towels and matchsticks,
Bound together with string.
He would fly across this town and across
this night,
Past chimneys through clouds,
To a room,
To find you,
Sleeping tucked tight.
And he would kiss every single sleeping
sighing frown away.
He would gently hook your hair behind your
ear
And ward off dreams
darkened by loss and fear.
He would chase the nightmares away,
Back under the bed,
And whisper warm words
And when all's done and said,
Even through the distance of sleep,
Knowing his ache will never wake you,
Even though hope's hopeless,
He would love you still.

All these things I'd do,

If only I could.

Like if I could make you love me.

If I could make you love me.

If I could make you love me.

I would.

David Parkin

A Slice of Satan's Team

Criminal government's regime.
A slice of Satan's team.
Persecution of the Falun Gong.
Their peaceful life made deadly wrong.
So his organs they will sell them on!
His terror is running deep
His family fall and weep.
For the government want his beautiful
heart.
No longer his to keep.
He lays down on the surgical table
as adrenaline runs so unbearable,
making him shake.
He doesn't want to fall asleep.
The one where he will never wake.
Oh why does mankind let evil rule?
Minds, they can be unbelievably cruel.

Julie Stacey

I Missed the Writing Group

I missed the writing group this week.
It was raining cats and dogs,
then the feline and the canine flood
just vanished in the fog.

I missed the writing group next week.
My time machine was sick.
I may miss it two weeks ago,
if I cannot get it fixed.

I missed the writing group today,
You all thought that I was in.
What you have failed to realise,
Was that I switched out with my twin.

I won't miss the writing group again,
I promise and I swear.
You need all the support you can get,
so it wouldn't be that fair.

I'll come to the writing group next week.
You can even save a chair.
What do you mean half term, you're
closed.
That's it, finis, don't care.

David Rollins

The Haunting

Somewhere across the night
she whispers my name,
broken, stuttered but said all the same,
mumbled, muffled into a pillow,
absorbed by the bed,
by the dark air.
Past midnight's lonely clouds,
the moon's icy stare,
I, in my turn, call her name,
face, innocent and oblivious,
my answer always the same,
her name
is my answer.
With the morning and the alarm and the
tea,
the names are gone,
too deep in the night's restless sea,
we forget.
We forget, even, that we dreamt.
All that remains is a haunting,
of someone being lost to us,

of kisses missed,

yet somehow meant.

David Parkin

Don't Play Ouija (True Story)

My Grandma told me of her dream.
A cross hung in the sky.
"Don't play Ouija," a voice boomed from
up high.
But what warning could stop an
adventurous teen,
in something they are so very keen.
And the story that follows is
true,
I tell no lie.
Now there's not many years
between my aunt Gail and I.
"Come round on Friday," she
said.
let's give it a try.
It was a warm summer's evening
when we took our seat.
Hoping spirits were here to greet.
An hour passed, the glass didn't move, as
we sat there so patiently,
the spirits it seemed would remain aloof.
However our disappointment was soon

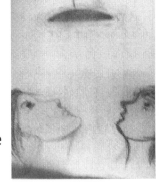

dissolved,
with a mystical quiz,
never to be solved.
The lightshade above began to revolve.

Physics in action is what we saw.
Going against its scientific law,
as we sat there in total awe.
It waltzed with its freedom
around the light.
Giving us such a delightful sight
and a belief in another world.
Maybe the mystics are right.

Julie Stacey

Pic by Julie Stacey

The Aeroplane, The Dream

Nose pressed against windowpane,
Watching the plane,
Imagining the dream,
Under the wing,
Clinging to the fuselage
In the ice-white roar.
Through the window,
Across the sky,
We saw
(Eyes squinting against the sun)
The flight,
Silently leaving a breadcrumb trail,
Spooling a twine
Against the blue.
The engine's lagging hum
Gently sung,
Of picking crumbs
And coiling string,
Chasing dreams
Under an aeroplane's wing.

David Parkin

ABOUT THE AUTHORS

David Rollins has now written several books for children and remains a loving Haiku poet. Having previously been a lunatic, care manager, social worker, library assistant and child there's a fair few books and poems left to write.

Julie first began writing poetry during a manic phrase of bipolar in 2018. These were published the following year in her first book "Journey of the Mad". Through poetry she describes the heights and depths of bipolar and her spiritual beliefs, which have their roots in the highs of this condition. She also includes a few supernatural experience's, although at times creepy, have offered her hope and an interest in a plane of existence, after death.

David Parkin is an author, theatre maker, musician and installation artist. His work is fiercely biographical, weird and wonderful, sublime and speculative, from his (award nominated) children's book and musical 'The Nose That Nobody Picked' to 'David Parkin's Delusions of Grandeur', an installation looking at the four months he spent under section, suffering from a bipolar manic episode.
Whatever the medium, his work is always thoughtful, moving and funny.

For details of our other books, or to submit your own manuscript please visit
www.green-cat.co

Printed in Great Britain
by Amazon

60420624R00064